Zero Is a Number

poems by

Michael Hammerle

Finishing Line Press
Georgetown, Kentucky

Zero Is a Number

Copyright © 2023 by Michael Hammerle
ISBN 979-8-88838-415-2 First Edition
All rights reserved under International and Pan-American Copyright Conventions. No part of this book may be reproduced in any manner whatsoever without written permission from the publisher, except in the case of brief quotations embodied in critical articles and reviews.

Publisher: Leah Huete de Maines
Editor: Christen Kincaid
Cover Art and Design: Michael Hammerle
Author Photo: Kirsten Hammerle

Order online: www.finishinglinepress.com
also available on amazon.com

Author inquiries and mail orders:
Finishing Line Press
P. O. Box 1626
Georgetown, Kentucky 40324
U. S. A.

Table of Contents

a.
01 | Carolyn

I.
05 | Staple in my Thumb
08 | Step-Dad Summers Buried Brothers Under the Bog
09 | Clothesline
12 | Where Was the Old Hammer and Wrench?
13 | I Swim
14 | Looking at my Son
15 | Tortic
16 | Dialysis: Lake City
17 | Child Mothers
18 | No Time Was Sacred and We Didn't Complain
19 | Symbiosis
20 | Hollow: A New Summer Tradition with Our Mother and Stacy (the Last Stepfather)
22 | Mistakes

II.
25 | Empty Cabin
27 | Empty Driveway
28 | Cardboard Kingdom
29 | Things I Learned Waiting in Hospitals
30 | Found Beauty
32 | Faraway
33 | Coin Purse
34 | Knife Collection
35 | I Used to Draw
37 | Old Woman and Tea
38 | Fortune Aground
40 | Cento anni
41 | A Father's Lessons Stick
42 | Age is Sobering
43 | Men at Twenty-Five
44 | I Compare Alexander in These Words and I do Not Apologize for Finding My Self

III.
47 | Possum Creek Skateboard Park
48 | When I Was Beautiful
50 | The World is a Barber
51 | Light and Heat
52 | Marineland
53 | Outage
54 | Somewhere an Exhibition Chef Takes a Break from Prep Work:
55 | Anonymous Obituary
56 | Push-to-Start Lymph Node
57 | I Should be Able to Move You
58 | There's Never A Good Time To Die
59 | Finite As the Body
61 | Dying
62 | Am I on the Island That's Thriving or Starving?
63 | The Virus I Am
64 | Salt Bonnet
65 | The Bastard I am
66 | The Good Stuff

IIII.
69 | Run Toward
71 | Some Boots Are Hard to Put on
72 | Hellman
73 | The Hell I See
75 | I'm One Man
76 | Work Clothes
78 | We Are the House We've Built
79 | Prisons

V.
85 | She has so Little Hair
86 | I Refuse to Breakdown
89 | He Will Rest When She Rests
90 | On Being a Child Who Lost Their Gone-Too-Soon Parent and Believing When the Other Parent Passes There Will Be Closure Only to Find the Placekeeper in This Tragedy Is Me:
92 | No Matter How Many Problems, It's One Burden
93 | Complimentary
94 | When I Had You All to Myself
97 | Acknowledgments
99 | About the Author

For Kirsten Faith Hammerle, Aurora, Calder, and Lakey.

...reasons to live.
—Amy Hempel

a.

Carolyn

(A poem for Gram and Pop)

say 'lo there won't you?
If you see me in the mist
young, strong, and happy.
Every night since
I've slept in the thick silk grass.
Truly under the stars—
I awake each morning and walk
the world over.
I watch you wake.
You stop in our spots
back to the wind.
These are times you swear
you hear me say
'lo there

I

Staple in my Thumb

Our home was close to a skating rink
that was attached to an alligator farm.
And Pop did not react when Chris was making tea
in the coffee pot and spilled it down the front of him.

I had dropped a cinder block on my finger
and Gram poured peroxide on it.
Gram, to help me catch my breath,
told me the commotion was the germs dying.

Pop only showed emotion when we ran
away from him and he had to chase us.
I had a staple in my thumb nail and
wouldn't let him take it out with
a pair of needle nose pliers.
He was pissed I was making a scene.
(Even if it was at home with no one to see.)
I ran past the pull-out couch that
Nana would use when she visited.

I crouched on the other side
and my Pop would only get so mad before he'd quit.

*

My cousins, my brother and I, had sat on the back of the couch leaning
into the wall and receiving temporary
tattoos by Iggy and my mother's sister.
The adults got real tats.

Later my aunt's children would set fire
to the room Chris and I shared—
It is still up for debate if her kids threw
the baby powder that was covering the room before
or after the fire.
I was so mad we opened that door
for my aunt's family because they treated
Pop's house like they'd never see him again.
I'd been to their house, a large studio, and they had

Mortal Kombat, but all the rooms were divided by sheets.
And there were too many snakes—
this is what I thought about all the time
I waited, side of the couch, staple in my thumb,
until my Gram got home to pull
the staple out.

*

My Pop thought I didn't trust him and that's not it.
My Pop worked on me like I didn't have
any damn sense of feelings.
Gram would give me a story and go
easy.

Pop worked me so hard I had to pretend
to need to use the bathroom so I could
catch a break. I had to keep up
with Pop or wonder if I weren't cut
from the same cloth.

My Pop accepted me back
after a neighborhood scrap
that nearly ended with my bike stolen.

Anytime my brother, Chris, and I fought
we had to know that you can't win
them all.

The lesson was hard proven
when a step dad and then beloved uncle,
showed us that blood runs slow
in the cold and beat my brother
in his ribs like he belonged
to no one.

My brother belonged to me
and I didn't know then to raise my hand
and share that burden.
The next time, I wouldn't need a story,
these situations would just be life.

If I had to pull the staple out
with my teeth, I could.

Step-Dad Summers Buried Brothers Under the Bog

Adolescence made a face hittable,
ribs so dig-able, to our step father
because my brother and I didn't belong
to anyone. We couldn't equal
the other child that never lived here.
We stayed away from Phillip
hidden among bald cypress,
water dried, and the land filled with dirt,
created tracks for buggies, Pop sent.

Abandoned construction site
obstacles, like concrete tubes, doubled
as a place to skate, or put a hole in the pocosin
hillside for Drano bombs,
trick learned from the swamp motel's handy man.
Bulbs lit up the backbox of the pinball machine
like a vanity and I could see
when my mom would visit him.
He had an office in the game room.
Phillip resented everything the handy man taught us.

For longer than not when I look at Ma, Pop, and Gram
They see what it took to make hunks of peat turn coal.

Clothesline

Chris, my big brother, had seen the bike thief
circle back and run over my legs.
I was feeling sorry for myself—
the wind knocked out my guts—
and didn't know Chris was right there.
I watched this kid-thief ride away gripping to hell
my gifted grave-digger green
handle grips and orange bike.
My big brother slammed his right arm
into the bike thief's neck like a clothesline.

II

My friend, he hid in a tree from the bully.
I'd been taught that only a softer metal
would blunt from beatings;
hardness begins
in the mind.
My brother and I "shared" a red bike
with a black seat and no grips.
He wasn't allowed to cross the street
because of where the street ends,
on the other side of the fence
is a trailer park: our first time over
we watched *Beverly Hills Ninja*
at a random kid's house.
Going home the group stayed strong
like a fifth and ignored the threats:
where y'all from, looking for somebody,
come hollar at us.
My brother too eager getting home
fell trying to ramp the ditch.
The bare handle bars nearly gutted him.

III

The time it takes a soggy wad of toilet paper
to fall from the bathroom ceiling on a seated,
arcade goer is about the same amount it takes
to chug suicides. Memories slippery as your first
step on a skating rink in rental quads.
The Skating Palace could whirl
like an above-ground pool at a birthday party.
Some skated the carpet and went straight to pinball
or *Terminator 2: Judgement Day* the mounted guns.
You had to get in where you fit.
Nice houses were closer to the roller rink
and Alligator Town. You could spot
monthly hotel renters by the work boots turned
upside down exhaust from the ac unit drying them.
We lived in the first housing after the hotel.
My best friend had a backpack full of Johnny Quest.
He lived in the last houses before Skating Palace.
I asked him for his old bike on Christmas day.
He told me he was getting a new one.
His mom heard me on their front steps.
He didn't want to give it to me.
She guided the bike by its green handlebar grips,
black wheels rolled and orange frame floated
right into my hands.
My brother had strolled on "our" bike to my friend's house.
I walked beside my brother. *He's not going to give it to you.*
On our way back home, riding side-by-side
for the first time, we said nothing.
I couldn't hear his bike chain slipping.

IIII

We skipped school and ran wild
in our friend, Eric's house.
The parents worked.
We watched *Robocop*.

and took turns as the look out.
Other kids strayed too
and stole the red bike
from the front yard.
They threw my brother's bike
over the fence into their neighborhood.
We couldn't be seen until the bus comes through
The weekend began with one kid squeezed
until he told us where to find my brother's thrift-store bike.
Washers, dryers, and refrigerators, the kid wheezed.
Every yard full of junk, we opened broken
down appliances, most were full
of water, nests, and rot.
We found the bike in pieces.
Pop got us
new hardware and a chain,
but the pedals always had a little slip
after that, like the chain that was on it was the only one
on earth that fit it.
Those kids even stole the black handle-bar grips,
and the Velcro, cross-bar pads.
Robocop still sucks,
but I can't think about him without remembering
Eric, holding a kid by the wrists
while my brother punched the kid in the stomach.

Where Was the Old Hammer and Wrench?

Brother, where was the old hammer and wrench? I can picture him,
flat pencil behind the ear and string chalk popping on wood. Grandma,
to prevent rust, buried his urn in an oiled cloth inside of a wax-sealed
shipping chest from a bonnet on a tugboat pipe. I can't stop the parallels
between a coffin closing and a tool-box clench (other than that Pop was cremated).
Brother, you took the weight when we were young and locked out.
That bought me a few precious years in the sound. Or I could just sit still
too with a small tell. We all know I wear my hubris in the pit of my stomach.
When my daughter was born, I could feel the switch. No more chasing
a father in Pop or you, but I did go searching for the lessons from the old
hammer and wrench—then you and I found less and less common ground.
It seemed that I only had your footsteps to follow but I didn't know when
you walked out you walked out toe-to-heel. As I was arriving you had
already left. Only with the birth of my daughter did I arrive at an adventure
before you, brother. When we had our boys a month apart that was the
real changing of the linch. We don't talk about Pop enough. After rescuing
the widows from their hoard—driving home—It doesn't seem like it but that was
seven years ago. Can we raise our sons like brothers fishing Alligator Lake?
Show these candies a neighborhood that's rough. Take the kids around, pieces
of a town our sons' great-grandfather built.

I Swim

in the back-swoller
of a shot glass
forgetting the clear cup was not a shot glass
but actually
a milk glass
and in the bottom were the remnants
of cinnamon and vanilla
not the ash from a little cigar.

Looking at My Son

Looking at my son
Pacifying:

I remember a hunger
Before ever remembering

An inability
To throw away

The things that have been
Until they are used

To the bread-scraping core
That learned hunger

Like the sun's light helps
An eye to develop

Adaptation
Survive off the (imitation) imitation

My son pacifies like a first-termer
Inconsolable

Tortic

Fathers' decide somewhere along the way whether they'll leave.
My mother was 16 when she had me, the second born,
my father was 24, moved her, after my brother's birth, to his home.
Irish twins was our nickname but we are mostly Welsh.
My mother was so patient so stoic.
My father just never came home and she didn't know when for leaving.
I was ten months when my mother lost us brothers.
Gram called DCF and they took us all to the group
where we lived until my mom was threatened culpable.
Us brothers then lived with our maternal grandparents.
Over the years, the courts would never deem her fit.
There are so many ways to lose custody for a mother.
We suffered infinitesimally. Pain that is macro acknowledged like tariffs.
When she'd married there was no better hull to their boat.
The stepfathers' sides, with a little spirits, were full of holes.
Never father figures but bigger bullies than a child
could hope to conquer without reaching a snapping point.
When she says it is the meeting of irons that sharpen the lambs—
that cuts deep like grandparents and courts were truthful:
seeing your mother too much is possible.
But she keeps coming back like optimism
offers cosset every day and wisdom.

Dialysis: Lake City

Dill pickle chips and Tijuana Mamas at 5:30 in the morning.
In-transit, Pop drives us to the dialysis center where he goes every few days.
Always arrived early and walked beside him rolling to his chair swap.
Later I'd wheel myself back to the lobby, GAME BOY on my lap.
Yearned for nothing. T.V. set to cartoons. Wheelchair parked
seat-to-lobby-chair for a bed.
Saturdays for years; three days a week in the summer felt like an abbey.
I was afraid-of-the-deafening-swirl-from-the-toilet's-flush years old.
Sly, had me write down his weight and lie.
Learned to love to push Pop up the steep, cracked concrete to the abandoned Sonics.
Crow's nest view. My mom's car parked. She was working at Wine and Spirits.

Child Mothers

If all the homes were creaking
would the fathers mind the floor
boards or would they
leave in their socks?

Our father could always return to
us, but like a true con
it's hard to turn
yourself in when no one can remember
your face.

Our mother, the living witness,
two-under-two by sixteen and left
for dead.

This house is his.

Our father goes
and waits
for us to leave
like we're the last electric
bill from a previous house.

We do go, I'm told,
after the food ran out.

No Time Was Sacred and We Didn't Complain

Terminator PinBall and Smashing Pumpkins
playing on the pool-hall jukebox.
When we were 11 (where'd we get the gumption?)
we'd set a roll of quarters on the billiards; call next.
We broke into the convenience-store ice cooler;
got on the roof and threw bags of ice to watch them explode.
Ventured out with the gas we'd siphoned from the mower.
Next-door-construction-site badlands like left-out au gratins.
We'd find bones and tar.
My cousin's dad had to give us a gasoline bath.
Rode that swamp go cart all summer like a first car.
My mother was the live-in night auditor.
We could hear the bell ding from the living room.
No time was sacred and we didn't complain.

Symbiosis

like a dog
that a seven year old handpicked,
a homemade go kart with a roll cage is
immaculate.
A child, one that hasn't been
corrupted, cannot perceive aged,
cannot see the faults,
only the fortune.

Hollow: A New Summer Tradition with Our Mother and Stacy (the Last Stepfather)

Deep in the coppice, the Catahoulas are champing
to fly out of their cages. Howling breath thawing the rime.
We release the hounds far from the cockcrows.
The badges on their collars briefly glint illuminated by
the red dawn sky. The Black-Mouth Curs never leave our side.
We all listen for the catch dogs; Staffordshires whine.
Keep the Laurels in mind my stepfather said as we footlogged
through the morass. He meant we should climb if we see a boar.

Days before, we'd took drums of motor oil and poured them
at the roots of the pines. The hogs rub their tusks there
and roll in the grime. We let the dogs trail the hogs' redolence
and follow their findings. The conditioned pack doesn't value
a shoat, conscious of consequence, of reward or ruins.
The game hides the sport. Always cold-hunt canines.
Trained in the forest, not in the fold my stepfather said.

We chose which dog would lead our first hunt
without our Stacy. We wanted Hollow, a mastiff.
The test: meet our stepfather where the gully is filled
with fallen trees. On that trek is where we saw our first cougar.
Its coatfrost flickered in the sun like flecks of calcite.
The eyes were eutrophic green like a cow field pond.
Hollow stiffened and lightly whooped to communicate
(his fat ruffled with the sound). The puma yowled
and bowed, and swatted toward the three of us. Maintaining
stance but a reluctance and hint of false-softness in its eyes.

Hollow charged and the lion wrapped around him. The two rassled
and the fracas rolled into myrtle shrubs. *Hollow* we said.

There was a caterwaul—my brother and I pulled each other
toward the sound—we stopped short and looked into
the shaking shrubs. Hollow emerged, rale-breathed, as he bled.
He was warm and wet in-between his shoulders. He had punctures
in his ribs. *Hollow* we both said because he'd lowered himself
to the ground. He yelped when we touched him and the pitch
of the sound was like a fork slipping on a ceramic plate.

Hollow was a brindle, one-hundred and twenty pound mass.
He rolled onto his side and his panting quickened.
A baying throng forked in front of Stacy and drove
down the holler. The pack circled the scene and Stacy
mushed them away with his boots and fell to his knees between us.
Hollow did not lift his head. His breath like weak wind
in a whistle played along to the laments of the Blue Ticks
and Leopard dogs. The Black-Mouth Curs were steady
and the Staffordshires, still nervous, were the only dogs who
circled. We apologized and whimpered, swore we'd never
go in the forest—never hunt hogs after—but we did
with our stepfather again and again.

Mistakes

Sowing seeds early,
that false, long sun
is like city lights
to some
fresh-hatched turtles.

II

Empty Cabin

Pop had a healed wound
on his throat—a perfect circle
where his father had trached
him with the empty cabin
from a pen he kept in his shirt pocket.
Pop was a man of short sentences.
My mother never found him
in any man she met
and Pop couldn't go back
and put the fire out that killed his sister.

Pop had eight brothers and sisters
but, after her death, he only stayed close
to one of his younger brothers.
Little thorns like a past due, wedding-band bill.
Pop's mother had said *use my account there on credit.*
Give me the money and I'll pay the bill.

He had quit school to work
a couple years before that. His first job
was the just-in-time shop with his father.
Cross on his wrist and snake on the ankle
he made my brother and I look him in the eye
when he told us that thieving is for lowlifes.

My mother was his middle daughter.
He and Gram had full custody of us before I was 2.
I think once his daughters
were older than "the sister he couldn't save"
he checked out.
My mother, pregnant by 15 and again at 16,
would have been in more trouble, but
she had had two sons.
Still, she didn't feel she could go back to her parents
and spent a year in the maternity group home.

Pop drank then, he quit
when my brother and I were in
Elementary school.

Empty Driveway

Gram was always working
the 11p.m.-to-7a.m. front desk
of the Best Western.
That's how I'd sneak out the house through the front
window and walk the streets just to do it—
no one knew, but my brother.
He "put a stop to it". (We were very young
and wouldn't have known to think Ted Bundy
had killed down the street.)
I loved the sidewalk, it was warm
on my bare feet even though the
sun had been down for hours.
It wasn't that I made the connection,
that my mom, years before, had gone
out this same window and altered her life:
Oh, I need to stop venturing out.
It was a game of tag and I wanted to tackle my brother.
He was standing on the couch
in the moonlight.
I flew at him chin-first. He hurdled
and I went through the glass smack into the sidewalk below.

Cardboard Kingdom

my grandfather made for us
out of left over moving boxes.
Doors that could swing,
windows cut out—
took up nearly the whole room
like Thanksgiving.
The memory was lost on me
until my nephew
stood next to his birthday balloons
and tumble house.
I could remember a place of comfort
and a realm within.

Things I Learned Waiting in Hospitals

Stick your finger in every coin recess
on any device and chase the almighty
two-fer. Walk around the hospital
enough and you'll find cash on the floor;
old ladies will fight you for the money
near the gift shop. The food court is the hotspot.
Only now that I'm older do I realize what
two kinds of people would leave, or drop, money:
rushed or careless. There's a mother somewhere who could
have taken her boys to the park, to the alligator farm,
to the arcade, to the skating rink, relieved them from
the place that teaches you to wait and select
what you hear, this one is for the grandmothers
that did their best, to families that walking side-by-side
is like a car, we don't hold hands when we cross,
but I follow my brother so close I step on the heel of his shoe
and piss him all-kinds-of-ways off.
The grandmothers' wheel the grandfathers, they look
like they are following
but they are leading.

Found Beauty

Found beauty in:
the lightning burst behind the tall,
dark buildings, that illuminated
the alleyways from the hospital
to the front street.

Found beauty in:
the heavy rain making a
grimy river spill into the drain
how everything may have looked
blue or that's just the way I remember it
now—

Found beauty in:
the ledge that went 'round the whole outer building,
and the doctor I imagined
smoking, crouched down there, daring,
and overlooking the ER bay.

Found beauty in:
going lower than the first floor,
even if the doors opened and the
terrifying word "morgue" was
advertised on the wall.

Found beauty in:
the dissertation summary posters
that hung the hallways' walls
like a movie theatre.
I'd appreciated every drawn-on
ceiling tile, I was starting to
give myself temporary tattoos with
a ball-point pen.

Found beauty in:
seeing brilliant people coming,
meeting, and going in the atrium;

watching doctors of all kinds
meditating over cigarettes and coffee
in the bamboo courtyards.

Found beauty in:
the food-court Wendy's line, where
soon to be widows' leather purses
wafted up comforting and steady, cold smells
that mixed well with French fries.
When we stood next to the doctors, they'd fold their arms
at their diaphragm.

Faraway

The tallest building in the city
a hospital—and my Pop
couriered room to room—
I took in the views
wondering suicide or accident
if the window locks failed.

Coin Purse

My Pop, coin purse by coin purse had anchored a giant Beefeater replica Gin bottle piggy bank to the floor. All the coins a life could collect. And two boys struggled to walk it onto a sheet and pull it into the kitchen to pour the change out on a blanket.

We'd laid the flooring as a family scraping the wood and cleaning it so the grout stuck and no tile shifted. The finished floor, we were sitting on it again like there was still work to do, but we were placing coins into a red coin counter that I always thought looked like a pan flute.

We counted just under two thousand dollars. Later, Gram went into town alone and cashed the change for bills. She paid the remaining balance of the mortgage with $1400 from Pop's change cache. She came back and got us and then we were driving south, I assumed to her sister's house.

We're going to the mall, she said. Gram took us to the stores we couldn't afford and the ones she hadn't let us go in.

My brother, my grandma, and I, we emerged that afternoon to the muggy, humid Florida with so many bags held by our fingertips we thought they'd pop off like hot dog slices. That trip made such a difference to how we felt that day. My brother and I were too busy tripping out about all the clothes and eating fast food, that we didn't even consider our next move was to return to our home once more. I can't remember what she did when we got back home. I just remember her coming to the conclusion that it was summer, she had a couple weeks off to grieve, and we really should drive to Orlando and be with her widowed sister.

I imagined the field mice realizing we were gone—eventually scurrying up the newer ramps we built for Pop to have easier access coming inside, and making their way across the brand new floors we'd laid as a family.

Knife Collection

We came home to check the house,
among other things,
and we did shut it all down and
packed the rest of our clothes.
There was no need for any furnishings
at Gram's sister's house.
Gram told us we could take a look at the knives
we'd inherited and we knew we really weren't
coming back. *Should we tell our friends*
and she told us that was up to us.
My brother did not interact with any knife
but his own buck knife and the colorful fish knives we'd
first been given: a few Christmases back, late
nineties, we'd unwrapped some gifts that were clearly
from the dollar store, fun, but nothing
like a TV-Christmas—we didn't let that show—
and Pop needed batteries for the train scene
running around the coffee table. He told me
to help my brother find the hurricane tote in the closet
and we found bow-clad, spanking-new tackle boxes and tool boxes—
fully equipped to bait cast, cast net, and build
a tree house from scraps—tape measures
so fresh we could stretch one across the room
before they snapped- hammers, nails, and levels. And in the top tray
of the tackle boxes were a blue knife and a green knife—
those two fish knives had made it back to the
8 inch deep, 4 foot long, tote full of knives.
Our inherited collection: some could cut bone,
some popped like a Jack in the box,
some spun open like butterflies, and there,
among a thousand stories, were our buck knives:
leather covered, black handled, and brass adorned.
We could take them with us.
But letting them stay meant we could admire them forever
like they were hand forged by Pop.
Gram had run her errands.
Soon the power will disconnect she said.

I Used to Draw

I'd clean the eraser
end of my pencil
dragging it on
any carpeted floor
or my jeans.

I'd draw murals
on the light-gray ceramic
desktops, or wood,
anywhere that took a line:
the white space of my shoes,
my forearms,
but never on a bathroom wall.
The desk art, I'd refuse to clean.

I can turn anything
into a metal cage
because of the time I found
that hole in the fence at the high school and fled.
I'd leave alone, but find
someone with the same idea.
The delinquents knew of a hidden pond
we could hang at a little beach.
Crouched along the cemetery wall,
careful about our sleeves and graffiti,
and crossed the street.

Leave at lunch and get a head
start.

When I don't graduate on time
I am the coolest guy
in summer school.
Self-commissioned Iron Maiden cover
On my desk and Mr. Long expelled me.
The Violent Femmes waiting
in a junk-green SUV.

It went lights down
in a culvert somewhere.
I climbed out of the back seat
and hung on the bumper
so the truants could flee the vehicle.
They were screaming my name.
My first instinct was to leave them too.

Old Woman and Tea

That boy's gonna' be
a heart taker.
He's got
our father's eyes;
rusty
like an ol' sunk ship.
He'll leave them girls
siftin' the wreckage
for something they'll never find.
Lord, he is just like daddy.
When's he gonna' stop
sugar coatin'?
When's he gonna' exchange
holding hands
for intertwined bands?
Get serious,
you know,
diamond dusted,
the hardwork.
Didn't he almost
lace his boots
once?
What was it he said?
That the ends were too frayed
and frail.

Fortune Aground

Born in Lithuania, Dela Palonis collected
Trail of Tears ceramic figures and dream-catchers.
She wouldn't talk past-anythings that weren't American.
1920, an 8-year-old child, on Ellis Island.
In her 30s, she married Grandpa Guy of West Virginia.
Dela, the second wife bore his second children.
John, her father, an only child,
while Dela came from a family of six,
it was important she collected.
Something about surrounding herself that was American.
Lining the shelves in her room with knickknacks
so many possibilities lost to her dream-catcher.
The barge cable broke and took the life of Grandpa Guy.
Something about surviving tragedies that's American.
Something in inventing uses
and personifying animals that's Lithuanian.
World Wars, the river, a daughter's husband
struck by lightning, collected stories
to pass from child to child.
The first time a family story is heard
guaranteed new like a child.
Curiosity like hearing Dela talk
about the Ojibwe and dream catchers.
She would tell us that the Native American had endured
pogroms and how they were collected.
She never talked about the Baltics
and the massacres that happened.
Nana felt safe
in West Virginia's mountains with Grandpa Guy.
Something in leaving her past omitted that is Lithuania.
Something in leaving her past omitted that is American.
Dela was a Transfiguration-church-confessing American.
The Hull Avenue Parish burned down
when she was a child.
Straight-to-Long-Island-City,
leaving-years-later-on-the-arm-of-a-soldier Lithuanian.
Shelves and birdcages circled her room in Florida.

So many parakeets that she never talked
about West Virginia or Grandpa Guy.
The birds had their own stories
every one she collected.
My Nana's children, two daughters, inventoried
her collection because listing is a form of grieving.
Then the daughters, and daughters' daughters, fought
for belongings as a show of caring
was so American it was English
and derived from Grandpa Guy.
Stories to pass from child to child a number
enough for each to take one dream catcher.
Native American culture to display
and remember Lithuania.
Dela, and her dream catchers,
our American beginning couldn't care to remember
Grandpa Guy or Lithuania.

Cento anni

The caramel sand of the beach
met gently with the blue water
in a way
that reminded me of Carmeli
slipping into that teal bikini.

Here the gulls cat call
like the neighborhood boys
as we walked
to the sycamore grove;
was that love then?

I've someone beautiful
and still I often dream of you
on my veranda
once again sharing
this same sun.

A Father's Lessons Stick

to a young man
like a sopping jacket
when it is
too deep to stand.

High moon,
tall reeds,
fishing with chicken livers.

Losing my inherited rod
and reel.

Too proud to call for help
we swam and waded
back to the ramp
shivering. I gave in

to the pleas of my squeaking sneakers
and I did not recover my lost pole.
Like sap on your palm
and pipe soot
are my father's lessons.

Age is Sobering

You can be drunk on youth; age is sobering.
One is a time where anything is possible,
versus, "Seen all—done all I will partner."
Coachella to cubicles and cost tables.
Serendipitous turned cynical.

What Cambridge is to Southies in Boston.
James Taylor vs. Aerosmith's *Walk This Way*.
Holding hands in comparison to rompin'.

Super charged with a heartland hemi.
Hybrid: half-electric / half-fuel.
Moore Demi opposed to Lovato Demi.
Seniority over new. A law. A rule.

Greenhorn jitterbugs gab until foot's in mouth.
Age, works hand overages fist to unbury the house.

Men at Twenty-five

After Donald Justice's Men at Forty

Men at twenty-five
dream through the night
sleeping when they can.
Days are for work, wanting
to fast break on life, looking for a layup.

Sharp as the knife of spirit—
cutting through the competition,
they have just arrived.
Enthusiastic like so many tender feet before.

Their legs are not yet fatigued
by those countless steps of validation.
But their heads are heavy
and the necks that carry are sore.

Men at twenty-five have just arrived
upon a stoop where strike plates hang
and through the door there's a steep flight of stairs.
You can't see the top stair in the dark—
when you start up
the stairs coo like a night owl.

I Compare Alexander in These Words and I do Not Apologize for Finding My Self

I

Bucephalus
died in Pakistan, no longer running
from his own
shadow.

II

I was taught to keep
the sun
in front of me.

No Phillip led me
to the words.

I was driven
by a ghost never seen;
and a ghost I haven't seen
for seventeen years.

No Olympia held me.
No title compelled me.

Any fears my brother and I had
never showed.

III

Possum Creek Skateboard Park

Like the emotional flood of a wounded veteran, with time, my ebb and flow had stilled as the waters deepened. I had to shut my eyes to remember my first time back at the park: without strength—legs that'd shake as if my limbs had fears of their own. How a weak chick approaches the edge of its nest, for a second time, hoping to fly for the first. Here the sun heats your back like the breath of a lover rouses an idle body from rest. I'm galvanized in the warmth like foliage after a fall night. Every stomp defies being a dead-horse limping. I ride here, fall here, I pick myself up, and I laugh here with my brothers. Tongue-wag grin, ignoring our aches like dogs. Other times I've walked here with a mother and buried Dusty's skateboard; with it a piece of me. I've broken myself here and built myself back up. We are going on without you, little brother. And I keep comparing myself to a veteran, seeing the gun shot, seeing my brother dead. The black suit framing him, his face and his hands for all to see, and the other details I will never say even though the words burn a hole in my chest and still won't fall out. There's an urgency to put into words and there's a guilt of having said anything. It has been six years and the story still doesn't feel like it is mine to tell.

When I Was Beautiful

(after Averill Curdy)

My being drunk by 10:30 a.m. was forgiven.
                              Wakeboarding
             on Lake Sante Fe.
Or surfing tipsy in St. Augustine
            teaching my "brothers"
                              to ride waves
before our little brother deploys.
                                        Mob-yap
                laughter like a box of scold puppies.
       First leave
                he took us carousing up in River Street
to a club with all his friends.
                              I could get away
with dancing by myself
                       when I was beautiful.
               How we met those French girls
                 playing truth or dare—
two running peach naked through Savannah, Georgia.
    Last call had passed.
                         The girls invited the three of us to their suite.
On the way home we schemed up
           next leave—
our brother had to be returned
                              like keys to a house being rented.
Dog tags were placed into his mother's hand.
                                  The family was last beautiful
                before the chaplain's knock
that no one heard.
                           In my sleep
                         I'm visited with images of my little brother
       so he's still living   in my imagining.
                     I think about promises
to tramp from Red River to 5th street.   I'd made good on that.
                 A set of dog tags around my neck,
         and stayed far from home.
Wound up renting a country house and proposing to a southern woman.

      There I could work in the lull.
                                          No mother's eyes
           that say we're less a son, now.
     No mother's hands.
No badge and no gun glinting in the sun
                                    to remind me
my being stoned by 10:30 a.m. was forgiven
    when I was beautiful.

The World is a Barber

A shaky-handed-straight-blade
stranger, smiling in my face.
The veil, the lather, and
spooling me around like yarn.
Halfway listening—preoccupied
with self. That I cannot trust
cutting so close to my throat.

Light and Heat

Death comes swift.
Just when the belly is full
and the coffee near perked.

Death comes for the babies—
the young, the grown,
and the old. More blind than gravity,

but as sure,
and experienced by all animations;
favors the unsuspecting.

A life can vanish
like tears from a windowbed
—photons, the stuff of light, radiating heat,
rose out the moisture—

as a good soul is said to
lift upward.
Time may be an illusion

but Death comes swift
when you are not the one dying,
and its wings ratchet
like the locust's tymbal.

If Death had a thought,
it was after the reaping,
and by design couldn't recall
a specific beyond its own hunger.
I doubt a conscious within/ speaks.

Marineland

(For Dusty, Gone too Soon)

Black-tip sharks swim straight and dolphins roll.
—Dustin Mitchell Powell

Walk off the sand bar, straddle
your board and paddle to the outside.
Post up. Throw some salt water
on your hot back.
The surface is smooth between sets.
Sunglint burns your retinas.
The pilot whale's dark eye.
Hell, why not drop in back door?
Explore the jetties, feel the fishtails
whip beneath your feet.

Outage

Random jazz
played from a battery-operated radio,
big windows opened
and the curtains drawn wide,
overlooked a pale field
the property enclosed with pines,

little moon high in the sky,
white sheets and candle light.

Laughed how it couldn't have been
any more fun
cleaning the old fishing cooler.
Filled it with ice and food
from the fridge for the week.

Kissed a woman goodnight,
who, save a white sheet, was bare
to stay cool.

Much as you'd of loved to
when she asked,
you didn't put down the pad and pen,
you sat and in your own way sketched—
fought sleep for a little while—
trying to capture all of the moment.

Songs segued,
stout candles burned bright
because their wax pools were shallow.
She was more beautiful than ever
for no reason

besides she had kept cool under pressure
as 1 a.m. neared,
with work in the morning
before sunrise.

Somewhere an Exhibition Chef Takes a Break from Prep Work:

stoop cold on the seat of his pants,
an apron, dusty with flour,
makes the wax-side of butcher paper all the more slippery
in his lap, damp palm heel of the chef's writing fist,
and his hand writing nearly illegible
on the opposite side of the butcher paper
with a grease pencil.

The pen slipping and causing messy long hand
because on the chef's thumb is a band aid.
That thumb is all agitated by meetings
with the sharp side of an old, paring knife.

Cutlery shaves towards the chef's heart,
the opposite of what he had been told
when his grandpa gave the knife to him.
The shank, brown from creating
potato quarters and cleaving the tops
and bottoms off, and julienning vegetables.

Hard to decipher could be a tactic
of the chef as writer, like his recipes,
he doesn't want scribblings to be read.

Anonymous Obituary

Mud-stained bedrock and resin floating,
Inlet I love for those cattail reeds.
Chew the heart of palm and no one is boating.
Here—inherited by the shotgun—we can sow seeds.
Arriving back to a place I was once from but couldn't remember.
End of the line; far as I'm willing to move my family north.
Last thing I ever thought was I'd get a letter in the mail:
Anonymous-sent obituary. The facade father's beyond the pale.
Anonymous constituary abused the trust they'd say on the nail.
Roused suspicion, and the greed, in me. The only thing I ever pined
Over was a woman and I had to know her well.
Necrosis acute or I'd likely disorder my stress to hell.
Hospital would be the last thing on my ever-lofting mind.
All out of sugar. I'm not over how I got the storking land.
Make them miss and take the piss out of their claim.
Mud-stained bed rock and resin floating,
Ear shaped swamp that drains and gloats
Restricting the culpability could I proceed.
Learned to look at the loch for its ability to form the creek
Eternally feeding my family.

Push-to-Start Lymph Node

A life like jumping out of a plane
with no chute;
falling for decades.
Push-start lymph node-
The body will find a way
out.
I've been all in
and want to stay at the table.
Hard to know
if you are a glutton.
Especially when the little biscuit just came.

I Should be Able to Move You

out of this house
but I can't.
I should be able to move you
with more than my words.
It ticks in my mind.
When I sit there is a guilt
stabbing my hip like a cramp.
I should be able to move you,
the baby, and these dogs to somewhere
else. We eat so well we could almost forget
the mold and the bow in the ceiling;
outside, the fleas in the dirt, sirens,
crime in the street.
I should be able to move you
with more than my words.

There's Never A Good Time To Die

I should be making 20-25 an hour.
I should have health insurance.
I should have had health insurance.
Instead I'm making 14-15 an hour.
Instead I have a sickness.
Instead I can't afford to live.
Stage 3 mourning-myself-and-I'm-still-here.
Stage 3 lymphoma
Stage 3 brain-flu-that's-actually-cancer
I should have seen it coming
but when you're poor all you have
is optimism—all you have is life
and when there's no life left
there's bills.
How a warm shower makes you feel better
my wife will bathe with steel wool
and my daughter will inherit that.
Liquidate me and the glass ain't half full.
We blame my employer for knowing
that a child needs stability.
I blame myself because growing up I was a child who needed stability
and that means I will take steady work over earnings.
You don't know what you don't know.
There's never a good time to die.
You don't know that you'd be saying *I'll pull*
the trash from the corner of the dumpster behind the hospital
and lick the bottom to see her graduate from kindergarten.
There's so many basic-human things I want
but here I am begging
to see my child turn 5.
In the back of my mind
is the thought that it may be more humane
that I'm going
while she can only say *Dadada*.

Finite As the Body

Here's a mouthful
of starches

and an eye-
full of tears;

a heart
to fill with smoke;

a heart
that beats slow.

Can't lift these hands
above my head.

Can't hold this numb head up
through another night.

If I could I'd eat
the tune.

Chewing
on a song.

I'd make it a sweet one
that'd split a tooth—

fork lightning
in my veins.

Loose this crick
that whines in my throat

and ticks,
tightening like ice.
Thoughts can be gems
or stones.

Either way you carry the weight.
Emotions for fuel,

that's finite.
water the bones. water the bones. water the bones.

Dying

We do it with our clothes on
so there's dignity.
We do it buck-naked
in frigid water.
We do it too young
where our parents can't find us.
We do it for attention.
We do it knowing it's the last time.
Hear my last precious thought:
I will take a journey
through a vacuum
because I choose to.
I'm not alone.
There is good conversation.
You are with me.
All smiles.
I can see us looking back
on Jupiter; and Earth
is now like a flint strike in the dark
of a cupped hand.
Say I do it first
this is where I'll be.

Am I on the Island That's Thriving or Starving?

For so long I wanted isolation. I wanted to endure—to be dropped on a desert island. I didn't care about the starving. I wanted to see the universe. People want the world but I wanted the universe. When what is tangible isn't what you want you live in isolation. Social starving. To be more you must endure. You cannot leave your island. Your starting point is where you are dropped. You can venture, or stay where you dropped. When the world is so predictable you look for the universe. The universe reassures your island. Rationalizes isolation. Says its best quality is its ability to endure; even when starving. You always know when you're starving and you can't find the other shoe but you know it has dropped. You wonder if you need contact to endure. You wonder if you can trust your eyes in this universe. There's no one to second what you've seen in isolation. Everything you dreamed is true about this island. You can't know how your wife and children are faring when you're on the island. If you'd brought your family they'd be starving. Are you still loving this isolation? What would it be like if you never left where you were dropped? If reality is fragmented across universes is there a dominant reality and that is the conscious that endures? Could it be that the last reality standing endures? All others are photonic projections of the same island; and therefore photonic projections of the same universe. Am I on the island that's thriving or starving? What would reality be like if I never left where we dropped? I had wished in every barren stretch for this isolation.

The Virus I Am

To suffer and see better company
puts a stop to the whole strength
like a scout hitting a trip-line mine

To ache alone is a warm blanket.
Knowing the pain will pass—biting on
a t-shirt because biting ladles buries each tooth backwards.

I think I learned
to suffer so quietly.
My head sticking out of the sand.
The whole of me is buried six feet down
like the virus I am.

Salt Bonnet

Peace
like a steady
paycheck.
When you are without
it,
every dream you had
harbingered
echoes
like the salt bonnet
fell off
in the soup.

The Bastard That I Am

I could give you a daughter
and try forever-love.
Hard to say
if I'm a good one
genetically.
I want to be so many things.
Tried more times than lightning
to be grounded.
Made more mistakes than all the lost
bastards.
Forgot promises
felt good on days
only because of my ability
to forget.
I could give you a daughter
and guarantee nothing else
but I'd want everyday
to not be the bastard
that I am.

The Good Stuff

goes out of your head
like a spinning quarter
Dog-Star twinkling
off the edge of a table.
The bad stuff stays circling
like Saturn's ice and strata rings.
Slow down long
enough and find the iron core
is magnetized.
After the fallout
see a starscape that hasn't been
observable for one thousand Halley revolutions.

IIII

Run Toward

I've never consciously ran away from anything in life, but I've found myself faraway from the things that could break me. I had been gone before I held my Pop's hand when he passed. There's little space between influence and choice even though I made the decision. But there was no choice that could carry me faraway when my daughter was diagnosed. I sat so still for that verdict my fingertips buzzed as they lay flat on my knees. I did not flinch, or twitch, or grip my jeans because I had that if-or-when grip on the situation.

My wife said that night as we pulled up to our house, our baby daughter asleep in the backseat, *these things break families.*

Come what may, I'll never run from this, we will pursue our daughter's health together. Because I know what it feels like to be ran from. And I know what it felt like to not rise for my brother once and then to run off to the city when my Pop was ill.

In that moment, when the diagnosis was handed down, hearing the neurologist, and exploring, the 3-D rendition of our daughter's brain, my wife intently focused on the neurologist's words seeing those facts, what I knew that I wasn't telling my wife, or anyone, was that I had these lumps: one in my arm and one in my back. And when we got a grip on our new-born daughter's health, I knew I had to go to the hospital. I dreaded that because it was the hospital Pop had all his treatments at (the same hospital where I was born).

I'd waited all year for the healthcare marketplace window to open, rather than be bankrupt, and got a PCP and so much blood drawn, then ultrasounds, such a familiar job to me, but I had never felt the warm gel or the remote slipping all over me and following my veins to see metastasizing. Headaches, black-spotted vision, just punch my ticket already. I've had life insurance all year—that's what Daddy can do.

Results: my PCP scheduled me an office visit to explain and my mantra through everything: if my daughter can be so strong, I can too. My wife knew as I walked out that the doctor told me all the things. My symptoms were not Cancer but growths, anxiety about those growths, and thalassemia. All that time playing roulette with my life because I could not go back to the place where I lost my Pop.

My two month-old daughter smiling at all the physicians, because it's new for her having to give so much blood, having every bit of her examined, intubating and MRI—she showed me how to endure.

I was lost on my way to have that ultrasound and happened upon where my brother, my Gram, and I had stood next to Pop—and we all had a quiet moment noticing a playground carved out a square in the city—I looked at the playground and the city and bounced between thoughts that I'd be OK, or, that this is where I began searching for holes in chain links. I bet myself that I stood here as a child and wished my mom would come get my brother and I and take us to that park. I believe this spot is where I began plotting my get away, and while there's no proof (because talent absolves) I was searching for an opening from my Pop.

    One wife, eleven years, two babies: I've found myself faraway from the things that could break me, like a little chunk of time when I was 12 years old, but here I am now, like I was then, (only I'm running from myself) learning how to make it right. I have to stand and deliver like a
young bride's optimism in her first born—like the love of a "first time father who knows the hurt of never knowing their own father". There's no coward here. There's only stillness and heart. Stillness until the fingers buzz and tell me it's getting time to share the weight of a story with my family.

Some Boots Are Hard to Put on

since they are hard to take off.
The work, hard-to-do,
you won't be able
to get out of it.
Like your child being born with a disorder
you find yourself.

Hellman

Last week I bought a jar of Hellmann's.
Usually I pass on it and say "Sorry,
Pop. I only eat Duke's."

I had been thinking about how he said
See you in Hell,
to people, occasionally to me.
As a kid, I'd be wondering why I'm in Hell
too to be seeing him there.

Pop was a good man.
And like me, that's never enough.
I had to know that *seeing him in Hell*
is an expression.
It was only funny
until he started to say it at home.

He was so sure
he was going
to hell that the silver pope necklace
on his tan chest was unforgettable.

I know now like surrounding
himself in Korean War documentaries,
boxing blood baths,
and buying Hellmann's,
he had juried, judged, and executed
his self-worth long ago,
when he fell off a building,
and lost his ability to walk.

The Hell I See

When I held my daughter's hand,
and kissed her forehead, as she woke
from anesthesia, the most recent time—
routine MRIs since
she was 6 months old—
she was 3 and
I was 30: I knew
the hell I'll see is in on earth.

My daughter's throat raw from intubation,
she couldn't drink so she had to have Popsicles.
Her mother rode next to the car seat
and I drove us home.
I should have got everyone something to eat
but after weeks of worry we all just wanted to get home.

My wife held my daughter in our living room
and gave her her first drink of the day.
I was in the kitchen making food:
I made my daughter a PB and J and
Turkey sandwiches for my wife and I.
I was fighting to be happy when

I brought the food into the living room.
If you are a Hellman, Pop, I wondered,
then what is that calm,
and cool, that permeates my heart,
when I was near bear caught,
on the side of a building with no shade,
for 8 hours, digging out a broken footer?

Something repaired me in the night when I begged,
Poppa, heal me. I was so close to heat stroke.
Who hears my daily wishes:
11:11 good health for my daughter.
And her feet stomp the floors
every dawn,

either just as I've watered the dogs,
or slept in and feel her
elbows and knees climb
across my body.

I'm One Man

But I feel like I'm two men, like a left hand and right hand;
smooth hand and coarse hand.
One man is hard, cusses like a bit lip,
chops wood and punches trees.
Throws the heavy bag across the yard.
The other man cleans and cooks his share,
loves his kid and never loses his temper with her,
finds his wife's favorite show from when she was a kid,
wakes her to breakfast in bed, a clean, dressed baby smiling
in his arm
and a plate of food in the other hand.
It is Mother's day.
She sits up and smiles, hair a little thicker looking from a night's
sleep
and the covers she tightens before they can slip down and says
thanks
like a woman who needed this
like we all need a little extra care sometimes.
When the man that is so mad comes out more frequently my caring
feels like an apology.
It is a balance like hanging your toes
off the edge of a concrete bridge.
That space under my heels is all I want left of the mad man.
I'm two men, like a left and right hand
smooth hand and coarse hand.

Work Clothes

Don't judge anyone
by the shirt. On their back
could be the weight
of their family's well
being.

Don't judge anyone by
the cuts on their
hands.
   *

Behind
their leaning
shed,

which leans because their dogs
have dug a cave
under one corner,

a man had kneeled
next to his crisscross-sitting wife.

A vibration
squeezed its way through
a thin glass window.

The vibration carried
a well-child's cry
and found its intendant
between the pool and the leaning shed.
   *

A man held
his enduring wife's
hand
and she said *Don't*
go
in the bathroom.

In the lap of her dress
was braided grass.
      *

She had quilled
a small circle bare
had not seen

a clay flip-flop key chain in the dirt
barely uncovered.

The man fixated on the flip-flop
and imagined when it was modeling clay:
an inscription
carved by a daycare worker,
or an exceptional child,
captured the child's will.

The man imagined if he held the keychain,
when it was freshly calcined,
his thumb could brush the words
(it was so real) those little ridges
they felt
like lizard teeth,
or pikes
on a Medieval crown,
and straddled the outline of a well-child's words.
      *

He brought buckets of pool water to their door.
The time: night rain. The grass was gauze
tied tight in a bag next to an empty pail.
Hurricane bands beating, like a tuning fork,
on the side of a hot house in need of power.

We Are the House We've Built

We love this house
because we built it
with our own hands.

We filled the house with light
and made sure our house overlooked the sea.
We are the house we built.
Slab and frame;
walls and roof.

We built it by the sea
and the sea is not always made of water.
A sea of Kentucky blue grass.
A sea of all the times we missed
each other. A sea that could be flat,
but this sea shimmers for every time we've laughed.

Every sea has its tides and beaches,
remember each reflection is a laugh,
and each grain of sand a hard time;
grains that make the beach—
we walk down to the water's edge
and say,

"I'll love you forever.
We are the house we've built.
We filled the house with light
and made sure our house overlooked the sea."

Prisons

Pop, my mother's father, had tattoos:
a green cross and a green snake.
I don't remember when those tattoos
became synonymous with his time in prison.

My biological father's prison was a prison of lies.
Lies can be more permanent than tattoos.
The lies he told, a scorned woman murdered him for those.
And his ink, I couldn't tell you if I inherited
a birthmark from him, let alone what he put on his body.

My first step-dad (the father of my sister) had no secrets
meaning more ink than skin.
When we came to his prison,
my older brother, my little sister, and me,
we'd dig by the fence with plastic sporks
and talk about how it'd be when he was home.

Talk to no strangers when visiting prisons.
Talk to no one at the vending machine.
When I piss by myself, because my mom can't go with me,
she says, *ain't no one in there*, but I'm scared anyway.
Hell of a lesson for 3rd grade to know Jasper
for its prison rather than its sports complex.

My next step-dad's prison was Desert Storm.
Tattoos of boots, with a rifle pointed at the sky,
straight as a flag pole, hung helmet, and dog tags.
All he knew was drills and kicking
our things into the wall,
and how to make my mother sleep
on the couch like a dog bothering him in the night.

We'd hear her there and give her compliments
until we all fell asleep.
He showed us all how to clean
a terrapin and make turtle soup,

black-water fish, pick the best dog
in a litter, and hunt hogs.

Desert Storm made sure my brother and I knew
how to ride in the back of the truck in the rain
for demanding he respect our mom.
I'd feel the truck slam to a halt
like when he'd kill deer with his brush guard.
I'd watched the man kill
and still I'd expect him to check on me,
but what he says is *make hotdog sandwiches.*

My last step dad is the most like the father
I lost: very particular, lets the spiders do their work,
runs dogs, just a few
low-quality tattoos. The difference,
"he doesn't want to be my dad,"
but he's the one at all my graduations.
Tied my tie before I graduated high school
and university. Tied my tie at my wedding because "he's better at it."
By the time my daughter can walk, he is her favorite.
All these things that were meant for Pop but Pop passed away
before he could see.

The time I do is vascular:
always making sure my daughter has
the ability to leap from both feet,
to speak.
The thought is there, a parent shouldn't
outlive their babies, I shouldn't have it
in the back of my mind, the real
estate on my body that I would give.
Please, Lord, let it be my name that's written.
It is no surprise I run
dogs, and let the spiders stay,
my tattoos, tell stories,
I only sit for them if it's like solitary, for hours.
And I pay cash. I know the deal.
This latest one is a stone ship on rocky bluffs

overlooking the sea.
I buried my father.
That's the way it should be.

v

She has so Little Hair

My mother's mother has so little
hair when she sits
in the rain at Walmart.
The electric cart barely fitting
under the canopy.
Her daughter and her car are headed
to Pittsburgh, or Miami, or Lake City.
After my wife and I call off our anniversary trip
and pick my mother's mother up, we spend
the weekend muting the TV,
so Gram can answer several police.
We are driving Gram to places the stolen car may be.
My grandmother's daughter is a felony stop.
The little time she has been out of jail
and what's all down her rap sheet.
The police are honest about how they are going to catch my aunt.
We have our baby in the car seat—
she keeps Gram distracted—
my wife is driving like a woman who's sick of being put out.
We arrive at the Best Western where
my gram had worked for twenty years.
I get out and talk with the police.
He, like all the other police, remind me that
it's not the best idea to bring my daughter.
Do they think we don't hate that my daughter is where she has to be?
There's no one else.
The car is a match.
My Gram's hair looks less thin when she thanks us and we go
in separate directions.

I Refuse to Break Down

There are two aged,
widowed sisters
using one's grandson
as a line of communication
like they didn't live through the tech revolution.
Even if the old ladies were wearing shoulder pads
when the word processors hit
the shelves,
as they say: *by 25,*
I'd been married eight years
and had three kids.
I see them
because I'm here
to be happy
like an old faded pennant.
(Gift from my grandfather.)
The one I see before I wake
my computer when I move my work chair.
One of them is here always
to see my children—so I hired both
to work alternating days for child care.
My phone buzzes and, rather than the old ladies look,
one wants
me to make sure
the other had turned off a pork roast.
Whether it is Gram or Jo, at my house they never bring a phone
like the oldest ornaments
are so surprised, so grateful, to adorn the new tree,
every year.
For either of these women to remember an obligation
to wear Nana's jewelry,
a burglar had to come one lunch and steal the whole jewelry box.
The thief threw a sheet over our dog, and
KO'd him with a meat mallet.
We had to have it stolen
before they felt robbed like the first year
those ornaments can't be put out

and then it hits.
I'm never getting robbed because I have all the obligations.
They leave their phones because they believe
they have no obligations.
I know them, could they, they'd leave all
and fly—only bring each other,
sodas, and meat cuts,
store-bought-fresh-baked bread and cheese.
All that they need
to curve a mood and be still.
And though they lean
on every boundary
and do not validate,
their leeds put the kids to sleep
and never let me forget the history
they both are very good at telling
and making reflexive.
They split the current
like a square boulder
in the middle of an old river.
How the body fails
and memories are like ant hills,
we don't know the ants are gone until
we traipse through them.
There *you* are:
worried about a little
rust in the coffee.
   II
I'm the old pennant
and my brother is the blank wall
with a really loud color
two coats down.
One of the widowed sisters once promised
me that a city was all I needed
to be an artist.
I never had the chance to choose
whether I'd be the old pennant
or the blank wall.
But if I would have known

my grandfather was dying—
that he'd die within the year—
I would have chosen to be the blank wall.
Being the pennant was "something brand new"
hung on the wall of a thrift store.
The grandfather, all that time ago,
where we'd went when there had first been no home.
We all were at the hospital, held his hand, when he passed in that room
but something my brother had seen
reinforced in him the wall—that his real self could live
two coats of paint down and he shouldn't look back.
I was gone long enough, only months,
but I learned that some are pennants so
bright they long to fade.

He Will Rest When She Rests

If my words are all
dead

is it because my Pop
died

seventeen long years ago?
No headstone.

But an urn in an oiled cloth
inside of a wax-sealed

shipping chest from a bonnet
on a tugboat pipe.

Shelf life.

And a spoonful in a locket
around his wife's neck.

Next year it will be eighteen.
What words then?

What new bit
will surface?

In what tone? Forgetting
is the cousin of really knowing
a thing
until it becomes a palindrome.

How else can I revisit
the kibble in the bowl?

What do we seek down here,
all that's left of a soul?

On Being a Child Who Lost Their Gone-Too-Soon Parent and Believing When the Other Parent Passes There Will Be Closure Only to Find the Placekeeper in This Tragedy Is Me:

Appealing to the fifth
wall.

Sifting through
the weeping

for the third
dimension.

In my family,
the lamented

rest
a little more

with each
placekeeper's passing.

Like the Cafe au lait
birthmark

that's been getting smaller
with every

fathom
of the family roots.

The tragedy will sink
into the trench

like an oversized wedding
band

turning over itself
in blueblack water.

Much as every heirloom is wanted,
the dive is its own risk.

No Matter How Many Problems, It's One Burden

We rent a white and blue house
on a little bit of land
where we can grow vegetables with no
fertilizer.
We grow tomatoes and peppers near the porch
by throwing our produce scraps
before it rains.
The trick is only shooting guns in the yard
when we have to (like the time that
seven-foot rattlesnake had cornered
the puppy dog).
We see turtles, bees, swallows, falcons,
and Barred owls, and I throw those owls shrimp.
I feel like a king renting this cut of dirt
because my son is crawling now
and he stops, sits up, and looks at me with the smile of a jack o' lantern
and we have a scream match
until the heirs jump out of the tall grass
and run past the dogs in the fence.
We've had a Clydesdale grazing in the front yard.
That's why I keep the grass long
so the horses come eat
and the deer hang by the pool.
It was love before stability
and stability came with good times.
Two minds
one burden.
No matter how
many problems, it's
one burden.

Complimentary

I got a cigar-serenade voice that is perfect
for telling the babies good night because
they fall right to sleep after. One would think
it's coming from a man with a Glasgow smile.
You've got a voice that's perfect for the porch.
I mean rocking in chairs singing old country songs.
The trees that had been blocking our view fell
during the last hurricane, cleared the skyline
and Mars is the red glow and Venus is orange.
I swore to you Orion let loose his arrow.
It was a comet, but you know me, I tell stories.
Like when I said we have 45 degrees of
compliments and 90 reasons why we shouldn't be.
But you know I see how we can stand in different
rooms and find each other in the mirror.
We can't look each other in the eye without
laughing or making funny faces. This world is built
for two. We are fond of each other like the poles
in a lean-to. Two triangles make a square.
Cut a right angle in half and those parts compliment.
I don't know what the hell we are but when you go
it's like forever I can only see a quarter of my
favorite painting. I need you, you spinning record.
It's you I want to hear all year and especially
at Christmas time.

When I Had You All to Myself

I did not know, for all those years,
that we would have our children.
You stayed by me and held me up
through the sickness. You were present
for the operations and took over
that one time for the medical assistant and
I knew then that I would ask you
to marry me. I couldn't get seen
by the specialist until after the wedding.
I remember us both crying for different
reasons. You because you finally
married the man you are "obsessed" with
and me, because God, let me see
my own wedding day and my daughter
with my mother coming down the aisle,
let me be
present for my bride
in her parents arms. You met me under the live oaks
at Doe Lake:
my son, safe in your belly
behind a blush dress, with a belt of lilac
ribbons, sterling silver strands, and pearls.
(I'd grown obsessed with you too.)

You had brushed my hair all those nights
and calmed my racing heart.
Assured me when my open-enrollment
health care kicked in that these lumps
was not cancer.
And I remember sitting in the car,
both kids crying, and you knew
by the look on my face it was not cancer.
Blood tests, ultrasounds, and a specialist—
it was not going to take me.
I picked a fight with you right there
because finding that I wasn't dying didn't solve all
my problems.

Losing our first son in gestation and
postponing our first wedding was still a burning wound.
Turning to you and asking if you wanted to book
the venue again so we could repair.
That was a couple days after we got those rainbow
flowers and visitors—
my brother saying he and his family are here
to support us through the unthinkable times too,
not just when we're up.
Still the words
we wish we never told anyone
so we didn't have to grieve publicly.

We booked our venue and I wished,
when I had you all to myself,
I could have been in that first year
what I am for you now.
I couldn't have loved you anymore.
But when I come in from feeding the dogs
and changing their waters, I wash up,
and I see you try to take bites of
your own food while feeding our son
and encouraging our daughter to eat
(who had just spilled her drink)
it always feels like I could love you more.

ACKNOWLEDGEMENTS

Thank you to Dr. Jessica Hylton for your endless guidance; thank you to everyone at the University of Arkansas, Monticello's MFA Program; thank you to family and my close friends for your belief, encouragement, and always being there for me. I also want to thank Bennington College and the University of Louisiana, Monroe, my time at both of these universities helped guide my writing.

Grateful acknowledgement is made to the following literary magazines and entities where some of these poems first appeared in earlier forms:

After the Pause: "Symbiosis," "The Good Stuff," "I Should be Able to Move You," "Possum Creek Skatepark," "On Being a Child Who Lost Their Gone-Too-Soon Parent and Believing When the Other Parent Passes There Will Be Closure Only to Find the Placekeeper in This Tragedy Is Me:"
Autofocus: "Prisons"
The Arkansan Review. University of Arkansas, Monticello: "Anonymous Obituary," "Am I On the Island That's Thriving or Starving," "Hollow"
Clementine Unbound: "Work Clothes"
Coffin Bell: "The World is a Barber," "Dying," "Carolyn"
Corvus Review: "Light and Heat"
The Daily Drunk: "I Swim"
Door Is A Jar: "Men at Twenty-five," "Outage," "We Are the House We've Built," "Age is Sobering," "Finite As the Body"
Dream Journal: "The Virus I Am"
Drunk Monkeys: "I'm One Man"
Eunoia Review: "When I Was Beautiful"
Foothill Poetry Journal. Claremont Graduate University: "Somewhere an Exhibition Chef Takes a Break from Prep Work"
Ghost City Review: "No Time Was Sacred and We didn't Complain"
Helicon. The University of Louisiana, Monroe: "Fortune Aground," "I Used to Draw"
Louisiana Literature. Southeastern Louisiana University: "Looking at My Son," "Tortic," "Empty Cabin," "He Will Rest When She Rests," "Knife Collection"
Misfit Magazine: "There's Never A Good Time To Die"
Mosaic Art and Literary Journal. University of California, Riverside: "Cento anni"
New World Writing: "Staple in my Thumb," "Child Mothers," "Empty Driveway," "Things I Learned Waiting in Hospitals," "Found Beauty," "The Bastard I am"
Close Up: Poems On Cancer, Grief, Hope, and Healing. Orchard Lea Books: "The

Hell I See"
Parenthesis Journal: "Run Toward"
Poetry Quarterly: "Push Start Lymph-Node," "Mistakes," "A Father's Lessons Stick," "Cardboard Kingdom"
Punk Noir Magazine: "Salt Bonnet," "I Compare Alexander in These Words and I do Not Apologize for Finding My Self"
Sandy River Review, University of Maine, Farmington: "Old Woman and Tea"
Shot Glass Journal: "Some Boots Are Hard to Put on"
Temz Review: "Where Was the Old Hammer and Wrench?," "Dialysis: Lake City"
Tendon. Johns Hopkins University, Center for Medical Humanities and Social Medicine: "Step-Dad Summers Buried Brother Under the Bog," "Faraway"
Terse Journal: "Complimentary"

About the Author

Michael Hammerle teaches creative writing and composition at a college and university. He holds an MFA from the University of Arkansas, Monticello, and a BA in English from the University of Florida. He is the founder of *Middle House Review*. His work has been published in *The Best Small Fictions, Split Lip Magazine, Tendon at Johns Hopkins, Michigan State University Short Edition, Foothill Poetry Journal, New World Writing, Louisiana Literature,* and elsewhere. He lives and writes in North Florida. www.mikehammerle.com

www.ingramcontent.com/pod-product-compliance
Lightning Source LLC
Chambersburg PA
CBHW020336170426
43200CB00006B/403